"Breathtaking." —*San Francisco Chronicle*

"The glory of the verse is matched by the exquisite illustrations."
—*The Baltimore Sun*

"Spectacular!" —*Chicago Sun-Times*

★ "A glorious, highly visual interpretation of the Nativity story. . . .
Readers will find this a work of art to be appreciated on many levels."
—*Booklist*, Starred

"A rich and memorable Christmas story." —*School Library Journal*

"Children of all ages will appreciate the visual and verbal delights
of this truly glorious book." —*Education* (UK)

"Vivid, dramatic quality, ringingly clear and timeless. . . . A treasurable
perennial." —*Evening Standard* (UK)

The First Christmas

The King James Version

with pictures
by

Jan Pieńkowski

Alfred A. Knopf   New York

IN THE DAYS of Herod the King,
the angel Gabriel was sent from God
unto a city named Nazareth, to a virgin
espoused to a man whose name was Joseph;

and the virgin's name was Mary.

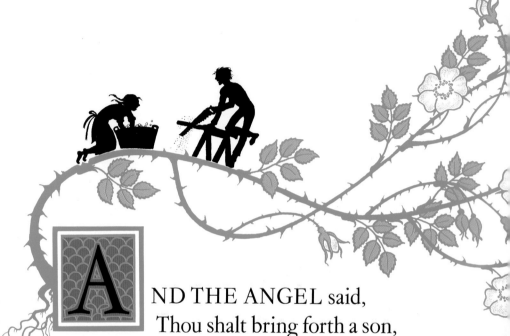

AND THE ANGEL said,
Thou shalt bring forth a son,
and shalt call his name Jesus. He shall be called
the Son of the Highest: and of his kingdom
there shall be no end.

And Mary said, Behold the handmaid of the
Lord. And the angel departed from her.

IT CAME to pass that there went out a decree that all the world should be taxed, every one in his own city. And Joseph went up from Nazareth to the city called Bethlehem, to be taxed with Mary his wife, being great with child.

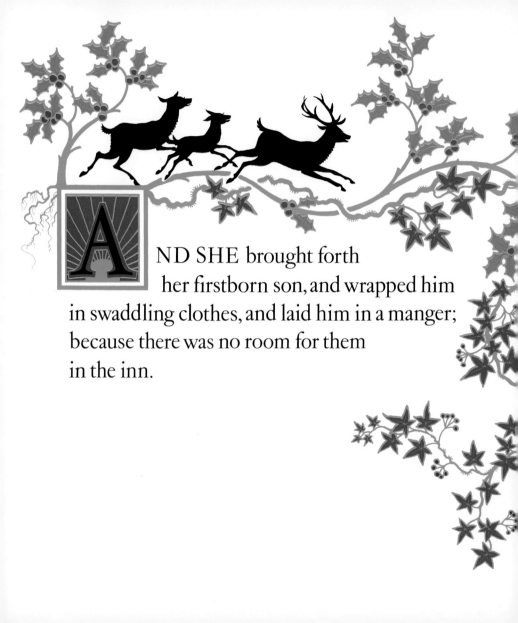

AND SHE brought forth her firstborn son, and wrapped him in swaddling clothes, and laid him in a manger; because there was no room for them in the inn.

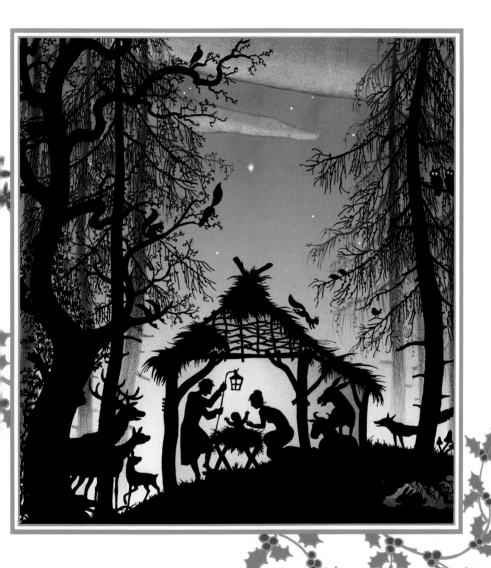

There were in the same country shepherds
keeping watch over their flock by night.
And the angel of the Lord came upon them,
and they were sore afraid.

And the angel said unto them, Fear not:
I bring you good tidings of great joy.
For unto you is born a Saviour, which is Christ
the Lord. And this shall be a sign unto you;
ye shall find the babe wrapped in swaddling clothes,
lying in a manger.

SUDDENLY there was a multitude
of the heavenly host saying, Glory
to God in the highest, and on earth peace,
good will toward men.

THE SHEPHERDS said one to another,
Let us now go to Bethlehem.
And they found Mary, and Joseph, and the babe
lying in a manger.

And all they that heard it wondered at those things which were told them by the shepherds. But Mary kept all these things, and pondered them in her heart.

And the shepherds returned, praising God.

EHOLD, there came wise men from
the east, saying, Where is he that is
born King of the Jews? For we have seen his star
in the east, and are come to worship him.

When Herod the King heard these things,
he was troubled. And he sent them to Bethlehem,
and said, Go and search diligently for the child;
and when ye have found him, bring me word again,
that I may come and worship him also.

WHEN THEY had heard the King, they departed; and lo, the star went before them, till it stood over where the young child was.

And they saw the young child with Mary
his mother, and fell down and worshipped him;
and when they had opened their treasures,
they presented unto him gifts:
gold, and frankincense, and myrrh.

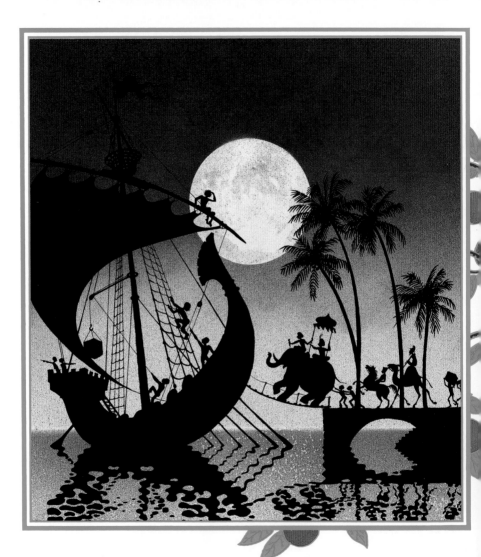

Being warned in a dream that they should not return to Herod, they departed into their own country another way.

AND THE ANGEL appeared to Joseph in a dream, saying, Arise, and take the child and his mother, and flee into Egypt, for Herod will seek the child to destroy him.

When he arose, he took the child and his mother by night, and departed into Egypt.

THEN HEROD was exceeding wroth, and sent forth and slew all the children that were in Bethlehem, from two years old and under.

Then was there lamentation and weeping and great mourning.

BUT WHEN Herod was dead, an angel
appeared in a dream to Joseph
in Egypt, saying, Take the child and his mother,
and go into the land of Israel: for they are dead
which sought the young child's life.

And he took the child and his mother, and came
into the land of Israel, and dwelt in Nazareth.

AND THE CHILD grew, and waxed strong in spirit, filled with wisdom: and the grace of God was upon him.

For my mother and father

THIS IS A BORZOI BOOK PUBLISHED BY ALFRED A. KNOPF

The following are extracts from the Authorized King James Version of the Bible,
which is Crown Copyright in England:
Luke 1:5, 26, 27, 30–33, 38; 2:1, 3–5, 7–16, 18–20, 40
Matthew 2:1–3, 8, 9, 11–14, 16, 18–21, 23

The illustrator would like to thank the following for their help:
Rowena Hart, Robert Roper, Hilary Saunders and Jane Walmsley

Cover and interior illustrations copyright © 1984 by Jan Pieńkowski

Visit us on the Web! www.randomhouse.com/kids

Educators and librarians, for a variety of teaching tools, visit us at www.randomhouse.com/teachers

Library of Congress Cataloging-in-Publication Data is available upon request.
ISBN 978-0-375-87151-1 (trade)
MANUFACTURED IN CHINA
September 2011
10 9 8 7 6 5 4 3 2 1